VOICES INTERNATIO

P R E S E N T S

The High Price I Had To Pay 3

FROM THE WHITE HOUSE TO FEDERAL PRISON

SENTENCED TO 11 YEARS AS A NON-VIOLENT, FIRST TIME OFFENDER

A MEMOIR

GWENDOLYN HEMPHILL

AFTERWORD BY JAMILA T. DAVIS

VOICES
INTERNATIONAL PUBLICATIONS

The High Price I Had To Pay: From The White House To
Federal Prison, Sentenced To 11 Years As A Non-Violent,
First Time Offender, Volume III

© by Gwendolyn Hemphill

This book is a real-life story about the events that led to the imprisonment of author Gwendolyn Hemphill. All names and events are true. The information in this book can be verified through public record. (See U.S. v. Hemphill Docket No. 03-cr 516 (RJL), U.S. District Court, District of Columbia)

Printed in the United States
First Printing 2014
ISBN: 978-0-9911041-2-3
LCCN: 2014942496

Voices International Publications
196-03 Linden Blvd.
St. Albans, NY 11412

"Changing Lives One Page At A Time."
www.voicesbooks.com
Edited by: Jamila T. Davis
Typesetting by: Jana Rade www.impactstudioonline.com
Cover Design by: Keith Saunders www.mariondesigns.com

TABLE OF CONTENTS

Introduction   7

CHAPTER 1 - Humble Beginnings   11

CHAPTER 2 - Labeled As An Outcast   17

CHAPTER 3 - Determined To Succeed   21

CHAPTER 4 - Destination White House   27

CHAPTER 5 - Political Socialite   31

CHAPTER 6 - Washington Teacher's Union (WTU)   37

CHAPTER 7 - Trial Versus Plea   43

CHAPTER 8 - Life In Prison   49

Afterword   55

ACKNOWLEDGEMENTS

First, I thank God for bringing me through this journey. Without God, my family, devoted friends and daily readings of Psalm 91 (my cousin Dorothy encouraged me to read it-she was so right), I could not have made it. Although I always thought I knew my purpose, God has revealed to me what His purpose is for me. I thank God for that.

Thank you, with my deepest love and gratitude, to my husband, Lawrence, for your love and support. I hurt you deeply and saw your tears, yet you never left me. May God bless you and restore all the years that we lost together.

Thank you Jamila Davis for your encouragement and help in getting this book done.

Thank you to my three great and loving children. Your love for me has been exhibited over and over again. And, to Michael, thank you for your support.

Thank you to my wonderful granddaughters. I miss our trips together. Although you are older now, we will continue where we left off.

Thank you to my sister-in-law, Eileen, who has stepped in as a surrogate for me. Your love and encouragement has strengthened me greatly.

Thank you to my sister-in-law Queenie and family. You are all loved an greatly missed!

Thank you to Donna for keeping me well informed about our family. Your words have encouraged me greatly.

Thank you to my three brothers. I love you unconditionally.

Thank you to my special friends Mr. & Mrs. Williams in church, who sat in the pew in front of me, for your love and support. You are greatly missed.

A special thank you to Pastor Terry Streeter, his lovely wife, and my entire church family at Mt. Pleasant Baptist Church. Thank you for not forgetting me and continuously holding me up in prayer.

Thank you to my relatives who have not abandoned me through this stormy season. To Rita in Pennsylvania and Yvonne in Tennessee your love, prayers and gifts have lifted me during many dark hours.

Thank you to my friend Mary in Pennsylvania who has shared kind words of support. Your words will never be forgotten.

Thank you to my special friend Pat, in Washington D.C. This has been a long journey, but you have stuck by my side every step of the way. Thanks for your gifts and your support. I am forever grateful!

Thank you to my spiritual leader Vanee Sykes. Your faith has been an inspiration to me!

Last but not least, to my friend Lizette, my deepest thanks for your inspiration and sincere friendship. Your support was never ending through the good and bad times.

To all of the angels God placed in my path, you know who you are, thank you!

God has truly blessed me with each and everyone of you in my life. Without your love and support, this journey would have been extremely difficult. Time has revealed your loyalty and your dedication. I appreciate you all greatly. May God keep you and bless you, and return the great kindness that you have shown me.

Greatest Blessings,
Gwendolyn Hemphill

INTRODUCTION

"Never in a million years would I have dreamed I'd be serving a very lengthy sentence in prison, as a senior citizen....What I've experienced was so harsh and so cruel that I wouldn't wish it on my worst enemy!"

My name is Gwendolyn Hemphill. I am a 73 year old, African American woman, currently serving a 132 month (11 year) sentence for Embezzlement, Conspiracy to Money Laundering and Wire Fraud. For eight long years, I have been locked behind bars in a federal prison, as a first time, non-violent offender. Broken and disheartened about what has happened to me, I've remained silent for way too many years. In hope to help correct injustice, I've decided it's time to speak out!

Never in a million years would I have dreamed I'd be serving a very lengthy sentence in prison, as a senior citizen. For the first several years that I was incarcerated, I remained in a state of shock and in despair. I couldn't believe that I'd be separated from my friends and family for so long, and left alone to survive in what at first sight appeared to be a jungle. What I've experienced was so harsh and so cruel that I would not wish it on my worst enemy! Consequently, for years, I cried many nights about my fate. It was so hard to fathom my new reality!

My entire adult life was spent serving my country and my community. I entered the world of politics with the hope that my contribution would help my people obtain their portion of the American dream. I fought passionately for justice, never figuring I would one day be a victim of injustice.

I went to trial with the belief that my true culpability would be apparent and I'd finally be vindicated. At the time, I had no clue what kind of battle I was up against. In a matter of moments, after my conviction, everything I worked so hard to gain seemed to vanish. I went from being an accomplished, well-respected woman in the world of Washington D.C. politics to a convicted felon. From that day, life for me has never been the same!

Sentenced to over a decade behind bars, I've struggled with my faith, trying to understand the purpose in my pain. As the years went by, I quickly noticed a common thread of prejudice that many of the prisoners around me also faced. Like lightning in my soul, I was moved to do something!

Last fall, a study was conducted by CultureQuantix based on the sentences of 29 female, white collar offenders, including myself, serving time at the Danbury Federal Prison Camp for Women. The results revealed that women were sentenced to 300% greater sentences than affluent white males who committed the same or similar crimes. That number was 480% for African American females. The results of this study were shocking! I was appalled! In a country that was premised on the ideology of equality for all American citizens, the results showed, when it comes to punishment we are clearly not treated equally. Should a white affluent male who committed the same exact crime as me serve less than a year sentence, when I am sentenced to over a decade? You be the judge!

This book was written to portray the truth and to shed light on a modern epidemic that has destroyed many families in our country. More and more women are being prosecuted and sentenced to very lengthy terms of incarceration. This disadvantaged population has been left without a voice.

The United States of America currently leads the world, housing the largest population of prisoners. Mass incarceration is a real epidemic that MUST be addressed! Tax payers are spending billions of dollars to house federal prisoners, like myself. In the Bureau of Prisons (BOP), the entity that houses federal prisoners, there are over 200,000 prisoners. Out of this population, 95% of us are non-violent offenders. It is less known that there is no such thing as parole for federal inmates. Therefore, we ALL must serve close to 87% of our sentences, which includes good time. There is no other recourse! Consequently, the federal prison system is 40% over capacity, "warehousing" increasing numbers of inmates for substantial periods of time. Many of us are women and minorities who are first time, non-violent offenders. Analyzing the facts and statistics, none of it makes sense! We need some brave Americans to step up to the plate and begin to ask the question: why does this problem exist?

On first sight, you may feel that the issue of mass incarceration does not directly affect you, so you have no interest. The truth is, one minor mistake could cause you to share a similar fate to mine. NO ONE is exempt! Therefore, I am sharing my story with the hope that it will bring awareness to this cruel epidemic and cause change. This decision was not easy. It was a difficult process to shed the many layers of shame and guilt that have held me bound, and silent for many years. As time has gone by, I realized God wanted me to become a voice to warn others about the severe consequences of poor choices and to speak out against over-incarceration. I have long paid the price for my crime, and have accepted responsibility for my wrongdoing, yet I still remain behind bars. Like many others, I am a victim of mass incarceration. After you read my story, I hope you will concur that it's time for real change! Please help to set us captives FREE! We need your support!

CHAPTER ONE
Humble Beginnings

"Even as a child, I was intrigued with politics. I took notice to the indifferent treatment of my people and felt emphatically that things needed to change...I never understood why the color of our skin made us unequal. In my mind, this just never seemed fair or logical."

I was born on April 4, 1941 in Johnstown, Pennsylvania, a small rural town located in Western Pennsylvania. From the moment, I entered into this world I emerged into chaos and uncertainty. Before I could take my first breath, I had to fight. Inside of my mother's womb, I was caught up in a battle between me and my biological mother, Rebecca Favor Thompson, who struggled to live as I was being born.

My mother was a strong, courageous woman. Like many southern African Americans, she migrated north in the 1930's from Camden, South Carolina to seek a better life. She and her son from a previous marriage, my brother Herbert, moved to Johnstown, Pennsylvania with my dad, Bennie Thompson. Through their union she gave birth to me.

From the moment I entered this world life for me defied the norm. Unlike most infants, I never got a chance to bond with my mother. And she never got a chance to feed me, change me or hold me in her arms. Within 30 days of my existence, my mother passed away. My brother Herbert, who was 12 years old, and I went to live with my paternal aunt, Maggie Wells, who raised us.

Although I entered this world under extremely challenging circumstances, my aunt whom I called Mama and her husband, my Uncle Ewin Wells, raised my brother and me as if we were their own. She had three other children, but she never treated my brother or me differently from them. To me she was my angel. She nurtured me with tender loving care and raised me to become a respectful young woman.

During my early childhood we lived in a row house beside the railroad tracks. The fourteen row houses that lined our side of the street were so close together that if one caught on fire they all would be burned down in seconds.

I grew up shortly after the years of the Great Depression. Times were hard during this era, especially for African Americans, who were called "coloreds" back then. Mama had a limited education, but she possessed great natural intuition. She was a stay at home mother and my Uncle Ewin was a worker at the Bethlehem Steel Mill. During those days most African American women were domestic workers who worked in the rich community of Westmont, and colored men upon graduation would work in the steel mill or the U.S. Service. My Uncle Ewin, who was very smart and gifted with his hands, worked his way up at the steel mill making a decent living. Therefore, my Mama did not have to work like most of the women in our town. This allowed me the privilege to spend a lot of time with her. Unlike the South, there was no segregation up North. Blacks and whites interacted together, but we knew our place. Although we made a better living than blacks in the South, the opportunities we had to advance were still very limited.

Even though I was raised by my aunt, my biological father, Bennie Thompson, still remained in my life. My dad was a tall, large man who had straight hair, fair skin and dressed impeccably. His dad was white and his mother was black. My father's skin was so fair that he could pass for being white. Back then, this had many perks. The light tone of my father's skin afforded him the ability to earn a good living working in a cleaner section of the Bethlehem Steel Mill. Some of the darker men worked hard shoveling coal into huge blast furnaces. This turned out to be a very dangerous job. Back then, they had no masks to protect themselves from the toxic fumes, and they'd come home covered with ashes. Years later, many of these men died from cancer as a direct result of working in such a toxic environment.

As a little girl, I absolutely adored my father. He showered me with love and affection. I can remember him picking me up early from school on several occasions to take me shopping. My father would take me to the best stores in town. There was this one particular store I loved the most called Glosser Brothers Department Store. It was the only store in our town that had an escalator, which was a big deal back then. Daddy would pick out the finest clothes for me to wear. I felt proud to sport the new clothes he bought me. I didn't have a care in the world in those days. Life for me was great and I was happy!

I also had a very close relationship with my biological brother, Herbert, who was 12 years older than I. He was an all-pro athlete and was very good in many sports. His talent led him to receive a scholarship to college, but he decided not to go. Instead he joined the U.S. Army. I remember when he returned home on a furlough from fighting in the Korean conflict. I was so excited to see him. Our family stood proud as he led us into Church that Sunday wearing his uniform. During those days there was tremendous pride in serving in the Armed Forces. Following behind him allowed me to feel a sense of pride too. At that moment I knew I also wanted to serve my country and be a hero, just like Herbert.

Looking back over the last several decades, technology has changed our lives. I dreaded Tuesdays growing up, because it was our wash day. In those days the women in our community used a wringer washer. The washer was pulled out of an alcove adjacent to the kitchen into the middle of the kitchen floor. Within moments our pristine kitchen was turned into chaos. Water was heated on the coal stove and filled with cold water for rinsing the clothes. A product named Bluing was placed in the cold water to "brighten the clothes," and on the stove was a pan with Argo starch to starch the clothes. Because the pan was kept at a boiling point, a stick had to be used to place the clothes in the pan, and to pull them out to be starched. The whole washing process was quite intense, nothing like today's simple washing machines. Nonetheless, when Mama went out to the dirt yard to hang her clothes, the clothes were so bright and white your eyes would hurt from seeing them sparkle. Washing clothes every Tuesday became a routine family ritual. I hated it!

Even as a child I was intrigued with politics. I took notice to the indifferent treatment of my people and felt emphatically that things needed to change. As I got older the differences of treatment between whites and blacks became even more apparent to me. Although we attended the same schools and movies as white children we did not go to their bars or their churches. I remember when my cousin from New York visited with us and we went with her to the local Catholic church (she converted to Catholicism after marrying a West Indian man). The entire service, the white faces around us stared intensely. It was so bad that I held my head down until the service ended. The stares became even more intense as we took communion and drank out of the single wine challis. I'm sure after we left the wine challis was thoroughly disinfected. I never understood why the color of our skin made us unequal. In my mind, this just never seemed fair or logical.

I also took note that every four years the "coloreds" in our town were momentarily treated as equals. During election time the "red carpet" was pulled out for blacks. The white politicians were in need of votes, so they would come down to our community to campaign. Their first stop was the McSwain's Restaurant & Bar. McSwain's was a black owned upscale restaurant with plush red leather booths and a long mahogany bar with spittoons. It had a large dining hall and dance area with a juke box that played all the latest R & B hit records. The politicians would come in the restaurant and declare that everything was "on the house." Food and drinks were provided free to all patrons, and the phony white politicians would mix and mingle with the colored patrons like they were one of our kind. They made promises to gain our votes, but after election day we wouldn't hear from them again. You would think these politicians would be despised by blacks, for making broken promises, yet they were greatly admired. African Americans felt proud to associate with the politicians, even though it was only once a year. I can remember my family getting dressed up to go to McSwain's to celebrate with these distinguished white men. In my mind, I thought this was ludicrous! I felt we needed one of our own in office to create real change. Even as a child I wanted to stand up for my people and fight against injustice, but I had two huge barriers to overcome; I was African American and I was a woman. Despite my obstacles, I felt like education would help me to achieve my goal someday, so I became engrossed in school.

School was my solitude. It made me feel important as I was learning things that even Mama didn't know. Not only was excelling in school important to me, it was also important to her. Mama had a limited education so she needed me to write letters to her family in the South as she dictated. I would also help her order clothes from Lane Bryant and pay her bills. This gave me a sense of pride, because I was needed by my family. It also gave me the inspiration to go to college. I wanted to break the barriers that stood between my family and higher education. I knew if I accomplished this goal, I could use education as a door opener that would take my entire family to the next level. Therefore, I was all in and I was determined to make a difference!

CHAPTER TWO

Labeled as an Outcast

"I was the little girl who never got selected by the team captains at school; no boy ever picked my lunch box at the church picnic social, and I was never chosen to be the bride at the children's mock wedding. I attributed my lack of beauty as the cause of my misfortune. I considered myself an outcast."

I was very happy as a young child growing up. Momma and my dad never missed a beat. I had everything a little girl could ever want. Life was perfect until I learned the truth.

By the the age of ten, I overheard a series of adult conversations that changed my life dramatically. My relatives would often sit out on the porch and gossip with one another. Approaching the doorway one day, I overheard them talking about me. One of them asked why my father spent so much money on me, and the other answered "because she is skinny and ugly; therefore he wants to make sure she always looks nice." On another occasion they also spoke about my biological mother being dead. Hearing these conversations, I was devastated! I never knew Mama wasn't my real mother, and I had no clue that my relatives felt I was ugly. Instantly, my self-esteem plummeted and I begin to cry.

After questioning Mama about not being my real mother, she simply said "How could I be your real mother if your father is my brother." I didn't dare question her response. Back in those days, children were expected to be "seen and not heard, so I ran to my room and cried uncontrollably. My world was shaken!

For many years I walked with my head down. In my mind, I was less than good enough. Consequently, I became shy, self-conscious and insecure. Keeping to myself became a routine habit. On the rare occasions I did associate with others, I always tried to please everyone in order to gain their acceptance. I was also super sensitive. Any little thing would cause me to cry. This gained me the title as a "cry baby." Quickly, I became accustomed to rejection. I was the little girl who never got selected by the team captains at school; no boy ever picked my lunch box at the church picnic social, and I was never chosen to be the bride for the children's mock wedding. I attributed my lack of beauty as the cause of my misfortune. I considered myself an outcast.

School work became my refuge. My teachers would often compliment me about my grades and my penmanship, so I worked extra hard to gain their accolades. I was always the first to volunteer to dust erasers after school and to escort a visitor to the Principal's office. I cherished the way my white teachers treated me. They helped to save the last bit of self-esteem I had left.

Life threw another spiraling loop when I turned 14 years old. My Uncle Ewin built a new house for us in the Prospect section of Johnstown. I should have been happy to move into a newly built home with hot and cold running water, a full bathroom, my own bedroom and no dirty yard or wooden porch for Mama to wash with lye every Saturday, but I was distraught! I didn't want to move and get readjusted in a new school around new people, so I pleaded with Mama to let me stay with my aunt. She said no so I had no choice but to leave the comfortable setting I had gotten accustomed to.

Mama was excited about the move. She immediately started a vegetable garden, flower garden and a grapevine. She would spend hours growing greens, cucumbers, green beans and cabbage. Mama spent the entire summer in a festive mood but I was in a state of panic. I tried hard to acclimate myself to my new surroundings, but I feared the rejection of my new peers at school.

As the summer neared the end, I approached my dad for school clothes. He had remarried and to my dismay he surprisingly said no. Instantly, he shut down. I never received anymore emotional or financial support from him. He was wrapped up into his new family. To me it confirmed the fact I was skinny, ugly and unlovable. In my mind, even my dad didn't want me anymore so no one would ever love me. That was another devastating blow that emotionally disabled me.

With the new expenses of their home, I couldn't expect my Aunt and her husband to take care of me financially by themselves. Therefore, at age 14 I received my Social Security card and started my first job. I worked as a live-in baby sitter on the weekends in the affluent part of town. This helped me to buy my own school clothes. After school I also worked at Glosser Brothers, the store my dad took me to on shopping sprees as a child. Working there I would often drift off thinking back on the good ole days I had spent with my dad.

The first day of school approached and I was extremely nervous. I left home to walk down the long hill into town where my school was located. It took me close to a half hour to get there by foot. As I entered into the Cloak Room of the school, which was dark, a boy grabbed me and kissed me. Taken off guard, I slapped him. Instead of being rejected, for the first time in my life I was accepted. The change I experienced was good!

In the winter of that year, I began secretly dating the boy who kissed me. He showed me love and affection that no one ever showed me. I believed in his eyes I was beautiful. This made me feel extremely special. For 3 1/2 years we dated and our relationship became intense. We both loved each other immensely. Mama didn't like the relationship, so I carefully hid it.

One morning during my senior year in high school, I threw up everywhere. I discovered this was due to morning sickness. I was pregnant! Back then, pregnancy outside of marriage was a total disgrace. When Mama found out she was extremely disappointed and embarrassed. She always told us "not to have her hang her head in shame." To my surprise, she didn't take it as bad as I thought she would; she blamed my dad for the way he abandoned me.

In the small town of Johnstown word quickly spread about my pregnancy. As I walked through our community I would often see the strong stares and whispers of the people. In church I was no longer allowed to sing in the choir and some folks instructed their children not to associate with me. Inside I felt terrible. I had made a mistake I could not correct. My pregnancy officially caused me to be an outcast. Once again, I was rejected!

CHAPTER THREE
Determined To Succeed

"Many people had counted me out and thought my life would turn out to be nothing. But there was an inner passion that fueled me and would not let me quit, so I defied the odds and pushed ahead!"

On June 21, 1959 I gave birth to my daughter. From the moment I laid eyes on my precious child and wrapped her tightly in my arms, I sighed in relief. My worst fear was that I would die after giving birth, just like my biological mother. I prayed to God every night asking Him to spare my life and give me a healthy daughter; He answered my prayers. This gave me a fervent drive to succeed in life so I could provide a good life for her.

After my daughter's birth I returned back to school to receive my high school diploma. My soul-mate and daughter's father, Lawrence Hemphill, was supportive all the way. He turned out to be an excellent father and provider. Directly following my daughter's birth we decided to get married. I was the happiest young woman in the world! Our only dilemma was we did not meet the 21 year old age requirement in the state of Pennsylvania to get married without consent. I knew Mama would not agree to sign the papers so I asked my dad to sign the consent form; he gladly did.

In September of 1959, three months after my daughter was born, Lawrence and I eloped. We kept our marriage secret at first and we still lived apart for a while, until I finished school. But eventually Mama found out and we moved in together. Starting our family life was not easy! My husband and I were young and inexperienced in raising a family. We had very little money so we struggled to make ends meet. After living in a small row house, we moved into public housing. Our rent was subsidized and we did not have to pay for utilities, so it was advantageous to us at the time. I quickly got into tune with motherhood and was happy to be on my own, no longer having to hide the relationship with my husband. Through our union we had two more children within three successive years. With three children to care for we needed more money to provide for them, so my husband enlisted in the U.S. Army for a four year term.

From the day he left depression engulfed me. I was 21 years old and alone with three small children to raise. Quickly, I became overwhelmed and my life spiraled out of control. I can remember staring at the wall for hours listening to Marvin Gaye records. During my husband's absence I missed him greatly. The fear that he wouldn't return often haunted me. My mind began to race and play tricks on me. One day while working at Bali Bra, a well known bra manufacturer, the whirring of the machine in the factory where I worked caused me to have an episode. I was immediately placed in the hospital and diagnosed with having a nervous breakdown.

At the beginning of my breakdown, I would see a woman sitting on a tree stump in the most beautiful forest with a bright light shinning through the heavens beckoning me to come to her. I would hold out my arms to greet the woman, but when I told Mama about her she would lay on top of me and hold my arms down to keep me from going to the woman. She believed if I went with the woman, whom she believed was my biological mother, I would die.

Three days out of the week, while I laid in the hospital, I had electronic shock treatments. This was a horrible experience! I was strapped down and a leather band was placed around my forehead. Then, I was zapped with the electronic shock treatment which would knock me out cold for hours. When I finally awoke, I would wake up with a violent headache. After several months in the hospital I was sent home for outpatient care.

Due to my illness, my husband was granted an early discharge from the U.S. Army and he returned home. After seeing him and my children, I gained the will power to overcome my ailment. Many people had counted me out and thought my life would turn out to be nothing. But there was an inner passion that fueled me and would not let me quit, so I defied the odds and pushed ahead!

Shortly after my recovery, my husband was invited by his sister to join her in Washington D.C. to gain better employment opportunities. She had taken the Civil Service test while she attended school and was afforded a good paying job in D.C. My husband accepted her offer and followed her lead. He also took the Civil Service test and passed, becoming an employee at the Department of Agriculture. A few months after he started working and was able to find an apartment, my children and I joined him in Washington, D.C. City life was a culture shock for me! In Johnstown, PA, the population was 90% Caucasian and in D.C. it was 90% African American. I had never seen so many black folks together in my life. The blacks in D.C. were different. They were a more progressive group that stood up for their rights and pushed to gain more opportunities for minorities. After a few minor adjustments to the new fast paced lifestyle, I fit right in! During this period I developed a deep pride in my heritage. Being amongst my own kind made me feel like I was a part of a thriving group that could overcome barriers of racism and poverty. This caused me to step up to the plate and take a shot at obtaining my portion of the American dream.

The cost of living in Washington D.C. was substantially higher than living in Johnstown, PA. Therefore, I had to work to help pay the bills. I had won awards for excellent typing in school so we rented a typewriter to brush up on my skills. Then, I took the Civil Service test and was hired at the U.S. Office of Educations, which later became known as the Department of Education. During this time we lived in northwest Washington because this area had a good bus line and we did not own a car. The subway did not exist at the time. However, we ended up moving to the southeast section. Back then, the newly built apartments were luring African Americans to this part of town. I was excited to move into this brand new apartment that had a lovely swimming pool inside the complex. To my dismay, the swimming pool was never filled with water and my neighbors began to throw trash over the balcony. Living there I was miserable and frightened for the safety of my children, so we moved to another apartment complex in Southeast. That didn't work out either. Eventually we found a house to rent back in the Northwest section and I was content. We had moved so much in the span of a few years that Mama asked me "if we were running from the rent man?"

Finally we had settled in and Lawrence and I began to excel. While working at the Office of Education, I enrolled in Howard University where I was a Political Science major. It was always my dream to attend college, now I was making enough money to pursue my dream. This made me very proud. Quickly, my husband and I made strides together, in our new land of opportunity. Our lifestyles substantially changed from living in a rural small town to the big city. We bought a nice home, our children were well provided for and we both made good money. I no longer had to hold my head down in shame, my success caused my family back at home to feel proud. It also gave me a sense of pride and dignity. Overcoming the obstacles I had endured, I knew there was no turning back! Deep down I knew there would be greater opportunities ahead and I was excited to explore them. My achievements gave me more faith than I ever had before, which filled me with a zealous passion to move ahead in life. I was determined to succeed!

CHAPTER FOUR
Destination White House

"From a rural town outcast, I passionately worked my way up to the White House doors! I gladly accepted my new position with great pride and joy. I knew God had shown me His favor and given me this position to make a difference."

During my tenure at the Office of Education and the Department of Transportation, I met a savvy, young man who headed the local D.C. chapter of the Student Nonviolent Coordinating Committee (SNCC) (famous for the boycotts led during the Civil Rights Movement). He called for a boycott on the the local transit system, due to the disparity of bus routes for Caucasian riders versus African Americans. I was instantly intrigued about participating in the boycott. Back at home, my parents had forbid us to get involved with the activities surrounding the Civil Rights Movement. I can remember Mama saying that we needed to "leave well enough alone." She felt that the opportunities blacks received in the North were sufficient, compared with the conditions she grew up under in the South. Personally, I feel the fear of losing what they worked so hard to gain caused them to resist advocating for change. As I watched on television my people fighting for their rights and being bitten by dogs and sprayed by water hoses, I became disheartened. I believed all Americans, regardless of color, creed or gender should be treated equally. The opportunity to stand up for what I believed in finally presented itself through the boycott, so I couldn't resist the urge to participate.

The boycott was a life-changing event for me. I was faithful to the cause. Everyday, even with a broken toe, I was present for the protest. Daily my passion was fueled even greater. Taking part in the activities inspired me in a way nothing had before, which gave me a strong sense of purpose. After this event I knew I wanted to do something to help my people in a greater capacity. It led me to seek out meaningful work that I would happily look forward to performing daily.

Directly following the boycott, I left my job in the government to work at a law firm in the private sector. While working at the law firm, I read about the great works of the American Federation of State, County and Municipal Employees (AFSCME), it was a thriving public sector union that was very progressive and politically active across the nation. I decided to apply for a position at the union and I got it! It felt good to work in a field I truly enjoyed. My hard work and eagerness to learn more about the politics of the union caused me to quickly excel and move up the ladder. At the time AFSCME was the fastest growing union in the public sector. The union lobbied on Capitol Hill and strategically positioned itself to be a reckoning force in National politics. It was the stuff I had read about in my history books in college. This was so exciting to me! The union's mission to help workers have a better way of life for their families inspired me. I emphatically enjoyed advocating for workers' rights. Every victory the union won pushed me to become more politically active.

During my tenure at AFSCME the union representatives were engaged with the plight of the garbage workers in Memphis,

Tennessee. They were trying to negotiate fairly with the mayor but ended with a strike. During the strike one of the workers was killed by a garbage truck and Martin Luther King Jr. was called in to help. We all were ecstatic to have King's support. We felt he would finally lead the union representatives to win the fight for the workers. I'll never forget April 4, 1968, which was also my birthday. It was a dark day for African Americans across the nation; Martin Luther King Jr. was assassinated. We lost a great hero. His death caused instant turmoil! Riots broke out across the country, bringing the nation to a sudden halt. For Blacks, King was likened to Moses. Without him leading us into the Promise Land, we were lost and in great disarray. King's death also greatly affected the union, who depended on his support. African Americans across the nation had to regroup and rebuild courage to move forward in the fight for equality.

Through my position at the union I was personally involved with the government from the Congress to the White House. Many politicians were endorsed by the union for election so we had access to key politicians, and they sought our help to gain votes. I traveled all across the country rallying advocators and strategically positioning alliances to help the union members. This caused me to become very popular and well respected.

After working for the union for 10 years, the union's Board of Directors endorsed presidential candidate Jimmy Carter. On a train ride to New York for a board meeting, I read his book and became a fan of Carter's. His ideals and principles led me to believe that he was just the right candidate to help my people. After reading, I made my mind that my next goal was to work for Carter in the White House. I immediately shifted into full gear working towards his election. I became actively engaged in campaign activities which included knocking on doors, working on the phone banks, assisting setting up fund raisers and organizing rallies in D.C. to increase voter support. My efforts gained the attention of key players on Carter's team, and even Carter himself acknowledged my drive after our face-to-face encounters at his campaign office in Washington D.C.

On election night when Carter won the presidency, I was ecstatic! It felt good to be a part of a successful presidential campaign. Shortly after his inauguration, I was offered a position on the President's Transition Committee. At first, my boss at the union refused to accept my resignation. Although it was a difficult choice to leave, I believed I could be a greater help to African Americans by accepting the position in the White House.

Working at the White House was a huge accomplishment. I walked proudly through the West Wing of the White House, ready to serve my country. From a rural town outcast, I passionately worked my way all the way up to the White House doors! I gladly accepted my position with great pride and joy. I knew God had shown me His favor and given me this position to make a difference. I quickly rolled up my sleeves and embraced the opportunity to be a liaison for my people. It was time for change, and I was ready for action!

CHAPTER FIVE
Political Socialite

"From the moment I officially became a part of President Carter's team my focus was to help African Americans gain resources and key employment opportunities. My desire to make a difference led me to become intensely engaged in White House politics."

Following the 1976 election of President Carter, I began my career working in the White House on the President's Transition Committee in 1977. The Transition team was responsible for reviewing the works of the Government and appointments to key positions. A short time after working on the team, I became disheartened by how few African Americans were appointed to these positions. As a graduate of Howard University, I personally knew there were many qualified African Americans, yet few were able to gain access. Back in those days, even the White House had very few people of color employed on the staff. Observing this deficiency made me passionate to help change the statistics.

From the moment I officially became a part of President Carter's team my focus was to help African Americans gain more resources and better employment opportunities. My desire to make a difference led me to become intensely engaged in White House politics. I knew I had to build relationships and set a good example for my people, so I volunteered my services wherever I could help out. Quickly, my skills were recognized and I began to make my way up the political ladder.

While working on the Transition Committee, I was appointed to serve as Assistant to the Vice Chairman of the Democratic National Committee (DNC). Numerous job requests came through the DNC. It was my responsibility to assist in referring candidates to the White House Personnel office. I was thrilled to have this position, which enabled me to help qualified African Americans gain employment. Through my position I scouted out rising stars in the Black community; aligning with old professors, friends and politicians, I helped to bring many qualified candidates to the table.

Shortly after working for the DNC, I was scouted out by the President's Assistant for Personnel at the White House, who was an old colleague of mine and had previously worked with me at AFSCME. She had consulted with me at the DNC to help fill several positions. My successful referrals led her to offer me a job to assist with Personnel Management. Through this position I was able to help even more African American candidates obtain employment. I also gained greater political contacts within the White House. Quickly, I became a rising star! Daily I intermingled with top White House staff who recognized my ability to connect with key figures in my community. I became a vital liaison between White House staff and the local African American community. It also gained me a position to work in an even more distinguished job for one of the President's top Assistants.

As a Political Science major, I felt I had graduated to the big league! I was appointed as an Assistant to the President's Assistant of Political Affairs. My office was in the prestigious West Wing of the White House. I was elated to have this position which helped me to gain access to the President and his wife directly. I loved the fact that President Carter embraced change and was open to giving more African Americans opportunities. Knowing his commitment and having his support inspired me to work even harder. With President Carter's Assistant's approval, I was able to help African Americans to gain inclusion in overseas business trips with the President. This was unheard of at the time, so it was a major accomplishment for Blacks.

My tenure at the White House served multiple purposes. It also helped in my personal life. I finally felt I had redeemed myself from my childhood mishaps. At one point, I was able to invite my Johnstown family members to the White House for a reception. They were beyond excited! They each raved about what they saw and continually asked "How did we get from Johnstown to the White House?" At that moment, I wished I could bottle my feelings of pride and joy in a capsule to cherish forever. Reality sharply sunk in! I had overcome many barriers that many said I could not achieve, becoming wildly successful in comparison to my humble beginnings. Reminiscing on my journey, I also stood in disbelief along with my relatives, realizing the depth of my accomplishments.

Supporting my community in Washington D.C. was another priority I held dearly. I worked intensely on D.C. community outreach efforts obtained substantial resources we needed. My efforts helped me to gain rapport with key political figures in my area. This caused me to become a sought after liaison to community leaders who called on me to help with community affairs. When problems occurred they would contact me and I'd take their concerns to the White House, and provide helpful solutions. It made me feel extremely good to know my help could make a difference. Every achievement I made propelled me to reach for even greater heights of success.

For Carter's reelection a campaign office opened in my hometown and I accompanied Mrs. Carter on her flight aboard Air Force Two to Johnstown. When my friends and relatives saw me standing side-by-side with Mrs. Carter, I officially became a Johnstown hero! I can remember the bright happy faces I encountered as I stood next to the first lady and waived at them. My nephew who was about nine months old held onto Mrs. Carter's hand as she greeted the community. It was moments like that which reminded me how far I had progressed.

Shortly after our trip, I was assigned to Pennsylvania to work on the campaign. I recruited several friends and family members to help out with campaign activities. It gave me great honor to teach them about politics and the election process. They were eager to participate and became quick learners. They vigorously supported Carter and recruited many others to do the same. While working on the campaign in Pennsylvania, Vice President Mondale also came to my hometown to campaign. My family and friends were honored and excited to personally interact with him. They would joke and say that I brought the White House to our front lawn, giving our small rural town new meaning.

As one of the the chosen spokespersons for Pennsylvania I would travel to remote areas of the state to speak on radio shows, which were extremely popular during this era. On one show, I specifically remember the host saying to me " I was surprised at how well you spoke." I was taken back at the time, but I became accustomed to hearing these sort of remarks as the campaign progressed. In the early 80's it was rare to see African Americans at that level in politics in Pennsylvania; and to top it off I was a woman! That was a hard pill for some to swallow.

We started off the reelection with a substantial lead against the Republican candidate, Ronald Regan. All was well until the hostage crisis occurred. American hostages were taken in Iran and tortured. Through intense media coverage, Americans saw the mistreatment of the hostages and demanded that President Carter take action. The President made several unsuccessful attempts to negotiate the release of the hostages and attempted a failed rescue effort. In what appeared to be overnight, in the eyes of the other nations around the world, our country appeared to be weak after the failed rescue efforts. American citizens also began to lose confidence in the President's leadership abilities. These events collectively caused President Carter to lose the reelection to Ronald Regan.

I was sad to witness the dissembling of the Carter Administration. As I carried my personal belongings out of my office in the West Wing of the White House, I flashed back on all that we were able to accomplish within a four year period. I had an eerie feeling that many of the efforts we had worked so hard to accomplish would be reversed under the new Administration. I knew I could not let this set back deter me from moving forward because my community needed me. I had already learned the power of resilience after losing the great leader Dr. Martin Luther King Jr., so I was prepared to fight. Once again I had another obstacle to overcome, but my passion and drive would not allow me to lose hope. I had comfort in knowing I was being led by a Force that was much greater than myself!

CHAPTER SIX
Washington Teachers Union (WTU)

"To me, my new boss was the kindest woman I had ever met. She gave me an opportunity to flourish once again, after years of a dry spell. I instantly made up in my mind that I would serve this woman wholeheartedly and perform my best to please her. She was my angel, or so I thought."

In 1981, after leaving the White House, I received a call from Marion Barry, the sitting mayor of Washington D.C. At the time he was having difficulties communicating with the local union representatives. Knowing my background and success with the union representatives, he asked if I would come and work for him as a liaison to the unions. I gladly accepted the position knowing it was an opportunity to serve my community and do what I was good at.

With the assistance of a few of my former colleagues, I arranged a successful meeting with the local union leader and the mayor. Understanding the needs of both sides I was able to help them come to common terms. After lengthy negotiations, both sides were mutually satisfied. It was a major victory for the city!

Through my position at the mayor's office I ensured that the city established and maintained viable relationships with the union leaders. This task was fairly easy and enjoyable to me because I was able to rekindle old relationships, which I had previously built working at AFSCME. Mayor Barry was extremely pleased with my services. He commented that I was one of his best appointments. My success led him to create an Office of Labor and Trade Unions during his second term.

I was happy at my job and things seemed to be quickly progressing. All was well until Mayor Barry resigned because of a political scandal that eventually led to his indictment. Overnight my comfort was snatched away. After the election of a new mayor, I was relieved of my position and relegated to an office in a back room; actually it was more like a closet with a rotary phone. I was crushed! I was so accustomed to being politically active and making things happen. Under the new mayor's reign I was completely silenced. Looking back, I should have probably scouted out another position, but the security of my well paying city job, with excellent benefits, caused me to stay. Consequently, work was no longer fun and enjoyable; it became a despised chore. I felt trapped and as time went by I seemed to lose my sense of purpose.

An opportunity presented itself for me to retire through an early-out option that would allow me to collect social security and get another job. I was worn out, so I finally left the Mayor's office in 2001 through early retirement.

In the latter part of 2001, I received a call from Barbara Bullock, the President of the Washington Teachers Union (WTU), a thriving five-thousand-member local union representing public school teachers and professionals employed by the Board of Education of the District of Columbia. Barbara Bullock invited me to attend a meeting in her office. I was honored to be back in the loop with those in my former field. At the meeting she offered me a job as her Assistant. I gladly accepted her offer. Instantly, I felt rejuvenated! Once again, I would be a part of a successful politically active union.

I adored Barbara Bullock. She was a strong, powerful figure, who stood 5 feet, 11 inches high. When she came into a room her mere presence commanded respect. For years she had successfully negotiated good terms for the union members, causing her to be highly acclaimed within her field. After working directly with her I became in awe of her savvy business sense. Her influence and her drive inspired me to become politically active once again.

A month after working at WTU my brother became seriously ill. Being so new at the job, I was nervous to ask for a leave of absence to visit my brother. But when I finally got the courage to talk to my new boss, to my surprise, she immediately agreed to let me go and presented me with a $2000.00 check to cover my expenses. I was surprised by her kindness. I asked her to take payments from my pay check to repay her, but she never did. From the moment I received that check my admiration and respect for Barbara Bullock skyrocketed. I've always worked extremely hard for everything I got in life. No one besides my husband had ever given me anything of such great value. To me, my new boss was the kindest woman I had ever met. She gave me an opportunity to flourish once again, after years of a dry spell. I instantly made up in my mind that I would serve this woman wholeheartedly and perform my best to please her. She was my angel, or so I thought.

As time went by, I noticed a number of personal checks were being written out of the Union's account and many elaborate purchases were being made on the WTU American Express (Amex) card. I acknowledged what was happening but I chose to turn a blind eye. In my mind, Barbara Bullock could do no wrong. This was my first mistake! My desire to be successful again got in the way of my conscience, causing me to lose my moral compass.

As I turned a blind eye, I was constantly showered with gifts and love. Over the course of a few months, Barbara Bullock became more like a big sister, than my boss; and we begin to interact more closely. At this point, she started divulging information about her embezzlement scheme and expressed that she needed my help to cash checks. Like a sucker I took the bait and officially became a part of her scheme. That began my day-to-day life of crime. Each morning I would get a call from my boss directing me as to the number of personal checks she would need and the amount. She created a rubber stamp for me with her signature, so I could write the checks and stamp them as directed.

At first, there was an accountant who worked for the WTU who was diligent about keeping the books straight. He would constantly stay on top of Barbara Bullock about the expenses she was incurring on the WTU Amex card. At one point he had the limit lowered because of her elaborate spending habits. Suddenly he died from a brain tumor and it was open season after that!

Barbara Bullock convinced me that I should take the position as the WTU's bookkeeper, even though I had no experience in this field. In addition to my pay check I would also get paid for keeping the books balanced. I foolishly agreed, giving Mrs. Bullock open reign to use the WTU's money in even more exuberant amounts. Whatever she told me to do, I did without debate. As time went by and her spending patterns got greater, I could no longer live in peace with my actions. Consequently, I contracted the Shingles and was out of work for a month. I believe that was God's signal for me to stop. I wish I would have listened.

The WTU financial state was in deep turmoil. Barbara Bullock had spent so much that she couldn't even afford to pay the union's back dues to the American Federation of Teachers (AFT), the parent company of the WTU. This was an urgent problem, because the WTU delegates would not be able to participate at the upcoming convention. Unbeknownst to me at the time, she had colluded with the Treasurer of the WTU, James Baxter, to devise a plan to generate immediate funds for the union. Instead of taking the normal $16.09 dues out of union members checks, they drafted debits for $160.09 to be taken out. This was their second time fraudulently inflating union dues. The first time their actions went unnoticed. According to court documents, this scheme was cleverly devised so it could be explained as a clerical error if they ever got caught. One union member immediately caught the error and complained. Instead of promptly refunding his money the WTU decided to ignore his request. That was a big mistake! This angry teacher filed several complaints, including a law suit, and eventually turned his complaint over to the Federal Authorities. That was the beginning of the end!

I had worked for this woman for a little less than 2 years and allowed my insecurities and clouded judgment to get the best of me. I had never in my life been driven by money, yet in a short time all the principles I held closely for several decades went out of the window. For gifts and bonuses of approximately $300,000 I had thrown away my reputation and my morals. I even got close family members entangled in my web of trouble. Now looking back, I realize how foolish I was.

When the court subpoenas and demands for all of the WTU's files came in, Barbara Bullock fled. She became a recluse. I was left behind to try and clean up the terrible mess that I had allowed myself to land in. It turned out that Barbara Bullock and co-conspirators had been committing fraud for five years before I ever started working for her. They managed to embezzle close to $5 million of funds from the WTU over a 7 year period.

In my 36 year career, I never had any kind of run in with the law. It took only two years to destroy everything I worked decades to gain! When the FBI showed up at my home, I knew I had a long rough road ahead of me. I immediately decided to come clean and patch up what I could. I had no idea of the backlash that this particular choice would cause!

Shortly after, our faces flashed all over the evening news. We made the headlines of papers, worldwide. Instantly, my name was smeared causing my family a ton of shame and pain. I cried profusely, wishing my life was over. I always seemed to be in control, but this time I had no way of stopping the fiery wrath that was up ahead!

CHAPTER SEVEN
Trial Versus Plea

"After consulting with my attorney who informed me I had nothing to lose, I decided to go to trial to try and prove my true culpability in the scheme. I was far from the leader/organizer the Government accused me of being, and a 10 year sentence seemed way to steep for my participation in the crime. Backed up against the wall, I felt I had no choice but to fight!"

After the FEDS intervened, I felt relieved to finally come clean and end my criminal conduct. I no longer felt indebted to Barbara Bullock or anyone else. I realized how severe my poor choice was to join in her scheme. I was dreadfully remorseful for my conduct and the pain I had caused my family. At that point, I was ready to pay the price for my actions and move ahead with my life.

I never had any personal experiences with the U.S. Judicial System, but I generally assumed the law was fair. Therefore, I cooperated with the law enforcement agents assigned to my case and confessed my wrongdoings. I believed by stepping up and accepting responsibility I would be shown mercy. I was wrong! When it came time to be offered a plea deal, I was given a 10 year plea offer. I was dumfounded! Ten years seemed like an awfully long term for someone who had joined the end of a long winded conspiracy. Even worse, I was given the same exact plea offer as Barbara Bullock, the WTU President who devised the scheme and embezzled over $5 million from WTU union members.

As I read the plea agreement I was surprised to learn that I was portrayed as a lead figure in the scheme. Not only was I accused of the activities I readily admitted to, I was also accused of many acts I had nothing to do with. As I studied the documents I became very angry. I couldn't believe that they had me on the same plateau as Barbara Bullock. This was unfair to me, so I challenged the Government's claim. After consulting with my attorney who informed me I had nothing to lose, I decided to go to trial to try and prove my true culpability in the scheme. I was far from the leader/organizer the Government accused me of being, and a 10 year sentence seemed way to steep for my participation in the crime. Backed up against the wall, I felt I had no choice but to fight!

From the onset I was in an uphill battle! With the swarms of negative press my case received in the media it was almost impossible to get a fair trial in Washington D.C. My attorney requested a change of venue, but we were denied. I was left to stand trial in D.C. along with the WTU Treasurer and the WTU latest accountant.

My trial begin on May 31, 2005. As I approached the court room steps I was met by the media, who attempted to ask me questions. I successfully pushed passed the cameras to enter the packed court room. Looking at the painful stares of my family members I immediately felt wounded. Day in and out, for three months, I listened to trial testimony about a woman whom I no longer recognized as myself.

Instead of being led and directed by Barbara Bullock, the story was framed as if I led her. How could that possibly be when this woman was embezzling money 5 years before I even began working for the WTU? The truth didn't seemed to matter to the ambitious Assistant U.S. Attorney who steadily aimed for a victory, at all cost. Consequently, I was painted as a monster who was driven solely by greed. My past political career also appeared to be held against me. It almost seemed as if I was punished for my past accomplishments. Listening to the testimony left me extremely confused and upset.

The most shocking part of the trial was to see Barbara Bullock take the stand. She was given a 10 year plea deal by the Government and was looking to reduce her time further by testifying against me. I hadn't seen Barbara Bullock since she had fled from the office and left me to hold the bag. In all my past encounters with her, she maintained a strong, confident presence, yet in the court room that wasn't the case. She appeared very nervous and avoided eye contact with me. Even when the Assistant U.S. Attorney asked her to point me out she pointed in my direction but looked the other way. I assumed her conscience wouldn't allow our eyes to meet.

On the stand, Barbara Bullock told many lies. She made it seem as though I cashed checks without her permission, for my own benefit. She also made it appear as though I brought her into the scheme. I became instantly infuriated listening to her false testimony! I realized at that moment I had been totally set up by Barbara Bullock. She had lured me into her plan, given me a rubber stamp to stamp her signature on checks, and made me a bookkeeper so in the end she could pass the blame on to me. Like a gullible fool, I had taken her bait.

It was a long hot summer in 2005 and I had a long trial ahead of me. There were voluminous financial files and checks presented to the jury. It was clear a crime had been committed, but it was up to the jury to decided who the real culprit was. My attorney did her best to present me in a good light, but the evidence and the fact I held the position as the bookkeeper was stacked against me. We could not show that I was innocent, as I wasn't, and the degree of my culpability was misrepresented by the fact that I willingly participated in the crime. Had I known what I know today about the law and our judicial system, I would have never chosen to go to trial versus taking a plea. I believe I would have had a better shot trying to convince the judge of the role I played at sentencing, rather than going to trial. Consequently on August 31, 2005, after a three month trial, in less than a few hours of deliberation I was convicted on all charges, even charges that were never brought down by the grand jury. At the same time, the new WTU accountant was acquitted on all charges. And, the WTU treasurer who was involved in the scheme from its inception, and who devised the excessive dues scheme, was found guilty on all charges but received less time.

Words can't describe the pain I felt when the jury announced the guilty verdict. During the trial I tried my best to stay hopeful, but the verdict shattered the last bit of hope I had held on to. I knew at that point, life as I knew it would never be the same. Consequently, I struggled for many months trying to understand the justice system I was entangled in. I never understood how the leader of a scheme could be rewarded for turning in smaller participants, when she invented the scheme. Everything I thought I knew about justice became distorted, causing me great despair. I was now a convicted felon, left to figure out how to survive in prison as a senior citizen.

With the support of my family members, friends and church family I prepared for my sentencing. Numerous letters were sent to the judge on my behalf. Community leaders and political organizations had vouched for my past works and character. As if I were present as my own funeral, all the work I had done was presented before the judge, with the hope it would help me.

For many years I was the President of the D.C. chapter of the Coalition of 100 Black Women, an active political group that addressed social concerns in the African American community.

During my reign as President we participated in numerous community outreach projects including housing and caring for many abandoned babies of crack addicted mothers. From Johnstown, Pennsylvania to Washington D.C., I had dedicated my entire adult life to helping others. Not only did I serve my community, I also served my country working in the White House under the Carter administration. Even after I left the White House, I was elected to serve as a delegate to the Democratic National Convention, when Clinton was the Democratic candidate. And, I worked for many years in the Mayor's office in Washington D.C. providing my service to the community. All my past works were presented and it was time for the judge to sentence me.

On May 22, 2006 before Honorable Richard Leon , in the District of Columbia, I was sentenced to 132 months (11 years) in federal prison. I was stunned. The judge had given me more than double the sentence Barbara Bullock got, who was ultimately sentenced to 5 years. Although she originally signed for a 10 year plea, her false testimony against me gained her a 5 year sentence reduction. And the WTU Treasurer who was a part of the scheme from its inception, and had devised the membership dues enhancement scheme, got a 10 year sentence. My sentence was the greatest of all those involved! This was shocking to me!

As the judge read his decree he stated I would serve 11 years if I was to live that long. He was right; the sentence he had given me was likened to a death sentence! It would only be the grace of God that would carry me through my punishment of over a decade behind bars. One of the reporters commented that it was like hitting an ant with a hatchet. I know my actions were wrong, but did I really deserve a 11 year sentence?

CHAPTER EIGHT
Life In Prison

"On sight of my new temporary living quarters, I became ill. Darkness hovered over my spirit and I felt as though I would take my last breath. I couldn't even cry; my pain surpassed tears. At that very moment I begin to pray. I asked God for strength, courage and the dignity to do whatever it was predestined for me to do behind bars."

I self-surrendered to the Danbury Federal Correctional Institution (FCI) on July 19, 2006 to serve my 11 year sentence, as a 65 year old, first time, non-violent offender. Because of the length of my sentence I was sent to serve time with the higher security offenders, including those serving life sentences for violent crimes. It was a culture shock for me entering the prison grounds!

I will never forget the sight of my daughter's tears as the correction officer processed me. In a matter of minutes I was no longer recognized by my title or accomplishments, I was now known as Federal inmate #27160-016. Taken away from my family into a back room I was stripped searched and provided with an orange jumpsuit, underwear and prison shoes. After I changed into prison garments, I was handcuffed and taken to the Special Housing Unit (SHU). This is the place where prisoners are normally sent for disciplinary actions. I was sent to the SHU because there were no available beds on the compound.

The SHU was a dreadful sight, likened to a jail scene I had seen in a James Cagney film. I was placed in a dark two-person cell with a sink and toilet in the middle of the cell, and a hole in the bars to slide a food tray through. On sight of my new temporary living quarters, I became ill. Darkness hovered over my spirit and I felt as though I would take my last breath. I couldn't even cry; my pain surpassed tears. At that very moment I begin to pray. I asked God for strength, courage and the dignity to do whatever it was predestined for me to do behind bars. As I prayed I was strengthened. I stood up and looked out the window and saw the most beautiful starry sky. It made me reflect on Saint Augustine's words "In my deepest wound I saw Your glory and it dazzled me." It also brought to my memory a piece I had read in Charles Stanley's "In Touch" Magazine, "The splendor of God's love gleams brightest when contrasted with the miserable mess we've made for ourselves."

For nine days straight I remained inside the SHU, where I was only allowed to shower three times a week and given one hour to exercise outside of my cell each day. On the 9th day my name was called and I was told to report to Unit 11K on the prison compound. As I exited the gated area to walk onto the compound the reality of the next decade of my life instantly hit me, and I became filled with anxiety. I stared nervously at the faces that surrounded me. The women I was confined with at the FCI were mostly drug offenders and immigrants who were being deported after they served their time. I had no clue if I would fit in or if these women would accept me in their environment. To my surprise, the women were very warm and friendly. Instantly, they began to help me. My commissary day was a few days away and I didn't have any hygiene items, so the women in the unit provided me with the items I needed. (By the way, nothing in prison is free except the food and board. All personal items including hygiene, extra food, sweat suits and even gym shoes and boots have to be purchased.) One woman even called me her mother and made sure that no one tried to harm or manipulate me. I was appreciative of the kindness that I was shown. It's like God sent angels to watch over me. They helped to heal my wounds.

After attending Admissions & Orientation (A & O), my first task was to find a job. Jobs are extremely important in prison as it is the place that most of your time is spent. I found out the Education Department was advertising for a library clerk, so I applied. I was called to the Department for an interview by a very friendly man, Mr. Menconi. After interviewing me he decided I should be a teacher/tutor for the GED program. I told him I never taught anything except Sunday School, but he insisted I would make a good tutor. He was right!

For seven years I served the Education Department wholeheartedly, helping many women from all backgrounds and walks of life pass the GED exam. It has given me great pleasure to see women, who were given up on, finally obtain their High School Equivalency Diploma. Dedicated to the cause, I was always kind and patient with my students. I even made visits after school hours to ensure they stayed current with their studies. As I believed in them, I took notice that the students began to believe in themselves. Many of these women were abused in their past and had low self-esteem. Some had never completed school past the third grade. I had to develop a formula to help these women pass the exam. My first task was to make them realize how beautiful and important they were, despite their past experiences. Then, I would work on helping them to overcome their fear of failure. After that, teaching was easy! During my tenure in the Education Department I was honored to receive a certificate of completion of the Education Aide Apprenticeship by the U.S. Department of Labor. I have also been commended by the teaching staff for having one of the highest success rates of students who passed the GED exam. I believe it is due to my formula.

In April of 2008, after my custody points were lowered, I was moved to the Correctional Camp. The Camp is mostly composed of white collar offenders, so I was now housed amongst more of my peers. In June of that same year my brother died. I was so hurt that I was unable to attend the funeral and would never see him alive ever again. I cried many nights about all of my misfortunes. After a while, I realized crying about my mishaps wouldn't help my current situation. I had to learn how to stay positive, even in the midst of adversity, and keep my eyes on the future. That is how I managed to survive.

In early 2011, I was pleased to join "CHOICES" a prison public speaking group geared to deter "at-risk" youth from committing crimes. Through this program I have gone into the community and spoken in colleges, high schools, group homes and at community events about the poor choices that led to my imprisonment. Sharing my story with both children and adults and witnessing their responses have given me new purpose. I realized there is an attentive audience who can benefit from learning from my past mistakes. Our group has received notable media attention and has been recognized by the U.S. Attorney's Office for the District of Connecticut for our community service. My participation has helped me to stay active in community affairs, even in prison.

At the Camp I am also very active in the Christian ministry. I function at the Christian Church Services on Sundays as the lead Usher. Through my position I've been able to direct many women to Christ, which has made me extremely proud. Despite my circumstance, I have refused to let go of my faith and my core values. God uses me as a vessel.

My greatest obstacle has been the absence of my family, who I've hurt so terribly by my actions. My husband who I've been married to for over 50 years has stayed faithful to me during this entire journey. The support of him and my children has been incredible to me. With the grace of God we have managed to weather the storm!

For many years I have stayed silent and just endured the pain I have encountered. I knew in this season it was time to speak out if I desired to help create change. For eight years I have been simply forgotten by most of the people I served all my life. Even worse, I realized I was not alone; so many of us behind bars have the same story! More and more woman are just like me, serving decade plus sentences as first time, non-violent offenders. We aren't all monsters as we have been depicted to be. We are women who made some mistakes, yet have provided sizable contributions to our communities in the past. Are our mistakes so unforgivable that we must be punished harshly? Don't we deserve a second chance? Are our mistakes so unforgivable? The tax payer cost to house us is exorbitant! Couldn't we pay our way forward in a more productive manner?

Even though I have encountered an extreme amount of hardships throughout my journey, I know in the end it will all serve a higher purpose that will bring honor to God. Today I realize I've been called to speak out against injustice. I have made a vow to God that I will commit the rest of my life to working to address prison reform. It is my desire to use the skill set I've learned behind bars to help women pass their GED exams on the outside and avoid prison. It is also my desire to tell my story to people across the world and warn them of the detriments of poor choices. If I could save just one life then my efforts will not be in vain!

It is my plea that you help me in my mission of advocating for justice. Please visit www.womenoverincarcerated.org and take a stand against the Over-Sentencing of women. Your voice can make a difference. We NEED YOUR HELP! Mass Incarceration MUST come to an end! How many more of us must suffer the terrible affects of its wrath? It's time for change!

AFTERWORD

Behind bars, I have met some amazing women. From a multiple Grammy award winning artist to politicians, lawyers and prolific activists, I have had the pleasure to integrate and learn from some of our country's most profound female figures. By far, Mrs. Gwendolyn Hemphill is a stand out in this group! From the day I met her at the Danbury Federal Prison Camp in 2010, she has extended her kindness and shared insight on numerous matters that have been essentially helpful to my own survival.

Having the opportunity to collaborate with Mrs. Gwen on this project and help her to share her story has been an extreme honor. She represents the backbone of our prison community! Through her strong faith and unwavering generosity she's assisted hundreds of women, like myself, in coping with the hardships of everyday prison life. She's one of the first warm faces that we meet coming through the prison doors and at church on Sundays, where she shares powerful inspirational messages that have sustained us through our journey.

Listening to the stories of women such as Mrs. Gwen, I instantly realized I was not alone in encountering injustices within the U.S. judicial system. Thousands of us have been thrown away and forgotten! With a plethora of undisputed skills and talents, and sizable charitable contributions, we possess the ability to pay our way forward in a substantially more productive manner. Instead, tax payers are spending billions of dollars to house us behind bars, where many such as Mrs. Gwen and myself are serving decade plus sentences. Left without their mothers to guide them, our children have been separated from us causing many of our families to be destroyed.

The average American citizen is clueless to the faces of women in federal prison and our stories. The shame and the intense pain our imprisonment has caused the majority of us to remain silent. With the help of leaders such as Mrs. Hemphill, we have jointly exposed our faces and hardships in an effort to create change- forming a powerful alliance and a new wave prison reform movement.

After reading Mrs. Hemphill's dynamic, heartfelt story it is my prayer that you will join us in our fight for freedom. Please visit www.womenoverincarcerated.org and sign the online petition to reinstate federal parole. Your help can make a significant difference! WE NEED YOU!

God's Greatest Blessings,
Jamila T. Davis
Creator of *The High Price Book Series*

Letters to President Obama
From Fellow Inmates At
The Danbury Federal Prison Camp
Requesting the Clemency of
Gwendolyn Hemphill

(Excerpted from her Clemency Package
Sent 12/10, which included over
50 letters of support from inmates)

Jayrece Turnbull
39915-037
Federal Prison Camp (FPC)
Route 37
Danbury, CT 06811

RE: Gwendolyn Hemphill Presidential Pardon

Dear President Obama:
    Every once in a while a light shines
brightly in the dark leading others to safety.
Seldom does anyone recognize the valor,
the courage it takes to inspire those in
despair. Ms. Gwendolyn Hemphill is that
light. For that reason, I recommend
Ms. Gwendolyn Hemphill for the Presidential
Pardon.
    Ms. Hemphill encourages inmates
to achieve their education goals. She
works as a GED Tutor in the Education
Department, here at Danbury, FPC.
Everyday, Ms. Hemphill teaches English,
Math, Science, Social Studies and most
importantly she positively reinforces
healthy study habits which helps the
female inmates to conquer their
prejudices from past experiences that

have scarred them, preventing the
women from believing in themselves.
Recently, I witnessed 11 women graduate
with their GED. I know Ms. Hemphill
was instrumental in their success.

President Obama please take a
moment and reflect on the following
questions. How would you feel if you
saw a woman imprisoned, trapped in
darkness for years (3 or more)
experiencing torment after torment?
What if that woman was you? What
would you do to help yourself after
being conditioned to fail? The answer
is nothing. Mr. President, you would be
paralyzed with fear. You would need
someone to guide you to safety. Ms.
Hemphill does this everyday.

Thank you for considering
Ms. Gwendolyn Hemphill for the
Presidential Pardon.

Respectfully submitted,
Jaylece Turnbull

11-10-10

To Whom This May Concern;

I'm writing this letter on behalf of Ms. Gwendlyn Hemphill. She is a kind, gentle beautiful person. She is currently a tutor here at Danbury Federal Prison. She has helped me personally alot. Everyday she takes her time to show me how to solve all my Math problems. I believe that she has Learned from her mistakes. I Also would like for you to consider giving her a second chance at life. She very well deserves it. I know that Ms. Hemphill will greatly appreciate it. So will I and I know that she will not stop helping people. She has plans on starting a school to help young single mothers. Which will help our community's, children & families will benefit from this. She has a bright future and a very big heart. Please consider her, As she continues to make this world a better Place....
                    Thank you Kindly.

                    Rose Caban #60053-061
                    33½ Pembroke Rd.
                    Danbury. C.T. 06811

Lucisita Santiago 28298-a
Federal Prison Camp
33½ Pembroke Station
Danbury, CT 06811

11-9-2010

Dear Mr Barack Obama, President of The United State

I'm writing you this letter on behalf of a wonderful woman who's name is Gwendolyn Hemphill. I had the pleasure to meet Mrs Hemphill in March of this year. Since then, she has shown me through her own actions how to follow my faith, continue my educational dreams and to look at this experience as a new beginning. She is a positive inspiration for all who knows her or of her.

Mrs. Gwen has never gone out of her character and has never turned her back on anyone. My heart is full of hope for Mrs. Gwen she has been in prison for quite sometime and still has quite a few years a head of her. She realized long before many of the women here the consequences to our freedom. She is good, true and a beautiful person who uplifts the souls of the women who are experiencing fear, hopelessness and the magnitude of their punishment. Our lives will forever be changed do to her kindness and amazing heart.

Sincerely,
Lucisita Santiago

11/14/10

Dear Pres Obama

My name is Patricia Graham
I'm incarcerated at the Federal
Prison Camp in Danbury Ct.
I'm writing to you on behalf
of Ms. Gwen Hemphill. I have
known her for almost five
years. She is like a mother
to me. I suffer from various
mental illnesses, and she is
always there to comfort me
and help me get over my depression
I'm also one of her students
and she works so hard to
help me and others. She would
be so helpful outside helping
women learn their GED so
they can make a living and
not end up in Jail.
Please grant her pardon

Sincerly Yours,
Patricia Graham
02827-084

Noviembre 9, 2010

Señor Presidente de los Estados Unidos de Norte America:

Mi nombre es Marisela Good. Estoy presa en el Campo de Danbury
Connecticut. Estoy haciendo una centencia de 18 meses los cuales
estoy por terminar y irme a mi casa. Le estoy escribiendo en
favor de una companera de esta institucion, Mrs. Gwendolyn
Hemphill, quien a sido una gran ayuda para mi en referencia
con la educacion que e adquirido en este lugar. Ella con sus
tutorias me ayudo pacientemente y asi pude pasar las pruebas
y calificar los requisitos y recivir mi GED diploma. Ella es
una persona admirable, querida, y respetada por las presas al
igual que las autoridades de este reclusorio.

Señor Presidente, yo le ruego que por favor otorge un perdon
un perdon presidencial a "Mrs. Gwen," como la llamamos de carino.
Yo estoy segura que ella por sus buenas cualidades es candidata
perfecta a recivir tal acto. Gracias.

                    Cinceramente,

                    Marisela Good
                    Register #31399280
                    FPC Danbury

11/9/10

Dear MR. President

I'm writing this letter on behalf of Ms Gwen Hempfill.

I only have good things to say about her. For instance, she is my tutor for all subjects as I was trying to get my G.E.d. With her help I did get it.

She is very patient, caring, dedicated, and committed to her students' success.

With her strenght of character, if would be beneficial to others out there. I sincerly hope you can pardon her. She really deserves it.

Sincerly
Marta Ramoz
12515014
FPC Danbury

United States Department of Justice
Office of Pardon Attorney
Washington, D.C. 20530

Dear President Obama:

It is with great pleasure that I write this letter of support on behalf of Gwen Hemphill. Respectfully I encourage you and the members of the Office of the Pardon Attorney to give full consideration to Ms. Hemhill's request for commutation of her sentence.

I have known Ms. Hemphill for a year, since beginning my incarceration at the federal prison camp for women in Danbury, Connecticut. Ms. Hemphill and I work together as tutors in the education department. It is a job that we both find fulfilling and productive. Because I teach english and science to the same students that Ms. Hemphill teaches social studies and math, I know first-hand the amazing impact that she has made in the personal and academic lives of her students. She is a highly respected, remarkable teacher that brings kindness and compassion in her efforts to educate a diverse and challenging student body. Her students love her and her effectiveness as a teacher is demonstrated by their newly discovered appreciation for education and successful understanding of the scholastic material.

Within the general population of women here at Danbury, Ms. Hemphill, or Ms. Gwen, as we affectionately refer to her, is a mother figure. Her life experience and maturity is often called upon in times of conflict within our community. Even during times when she is not feeling well due to her debilitating health, Ms. Gwen always avails herself as a maternal figure, mediator and counselor.

In light of the many research and study results regarding the negative impacts of incarceration, it is no more futile a form of punishment for older, first-time, non-violent offenders such as Ms. Gwen Hemphill. There are more productive, cost-effective, victim-oriented, restorative justice solutions to address criminal behavior, particularly aberrant behavior as is the case with Ms. Gwen's involvement in the criminal justice system.

Please provide Ms. Gwen Hemphill with your full consideration for the commutation of her sentence as she is most worthy and deserving of an opportunity for release to her family and community.

Very truly yours,

Andrea C. Goode-James
27402-038

Marsha Hoffman-Vaile # 31170-018
Danbury Prison Camp
33 1/2 Pembroke Rd.
Dambury, Ct. 06811

11/11/10

Dear President Obama,

I am writing in support of a pardon for Gwendolyn Hemphil. She very much deserves your Presidential Pardon.

I have been incarcerated over 3 years here in Danbury, Connecticut. I met "Miss Gwen " a year ago when i was moved from the F.C.I., Federal Correctional Institution, to the camp. She was one of the first friendly faces that made me feel welcome and safe. She was so kind and helpful to me and was so eager to make me feel comfortable in my new surroundings. She is such a considerate and compassionate Christian woman who truly cares about others. I could not imagine how such a lovely conservative and calm older lady could be incarcerated.

"Miss Gwen" keeps busy helping others, crocheting and knitting, practicing her strong Christian faith, and being a smiling positive influence to those of us who get discouraged and depressed.

I strongly feel she has served enough time in prison and needs to go home to family and loved ones. She would be such a a wonderful inspiring addition and Christian influence to any community. I have never seen her angry or heard her say a mean-spirited word to or about another person. She is the most unselfish person I have met here and truly deserves to pend the remainder of her "Golden Years" away from prison.

Sincerely,

Marsha Lynn Hoffman-Vaile #31170-018

President Obama,

I have been inmate at Danbury Connecticut Federal Prison Camp from march 10, 2010 until now. I met Ms Gwendolyn Hemphill here as a inmate, which she takes the time to teach in the education department. She takes time with each person to make sure they understand there lessons, so they can pass the Ged test. Ms Gwendolyn also a member of the Usher ministry here at Danbury. Ms Gwendolyn is a respectable, patient, humble person, which I ~~know~~ she would make a very good Cadidate for a Pardon.

Sinda Butcher
58529-083
11-9-10

November 10, 2010

To Whom This May Concern,

I am writing this character letter for Ms. Gwendolyn Hemphill. I have had the pleasure of knowing "Ms. Gwen" going on 4 years.

What started out as co-workers, has blossomed into a friendship. What attracted me to her, was her heart. She has always showed concern for others. Ms. Gwen is a very kind and caring person.

I've watched her go through some discouraging moments, but yet she still remains optimistic about the future. She's such a strong, positive and spiritual person. She is a woman with so much to offer, and given the opportunity all females can benefit from that.

Despite her current situation, nothing brings her down. I'm blessed to know this genuine, loving person and to have her as my friend.

Sincerely,

Monique Williams
07581-030

11-9-10

To Whom it May Concern,

I'm writing this letter in reference to Miss Gwendolyn Hemphill, who I've been incarcerated with for 28 months.

Since I've known Miss Gwen she has shown compassion and strength which are traits that are inspirational to all of us women here. I know I can always go to Miss Gwen for sound advice, she never puts herself first and goes above and beyond with her students to make sure they are successful and that they know they have tons of potential to do great things.

She's a wonderful woman who's made a big difference in my life.

Sincerely,

Rachel Reyes
57107-083

November 14, 2010

To Whom It May Concern,

I am writing this letter on behalf of Mrs. Gwendolyn Hemphill who is incarcerated in Danbury Federal Prison Camp.

It has been brought to my attention that she may be a possible candidate for a pardon. I believe that she's a perfect candidate and should be granted it.

Mrs. Hemphill is one of the eldest here at the camp. She's a very kind, loving and caring woman who's respected by all. She's available whenever you're in need of anything, whether it's something of monetary value, emotional support or help with higher learning. Mrs. Gwen, as we call her, is unique in character because it's rare that you can find a woman who attains so many positive qualities and the ability to be so patient and loving even under these circumstances.

Incarceration is a very difficult experience, and I am not aware of what

Mrs Gwen's crime is but I know that
she doesn't belong here. If anyone deserves
a second chance I truly believe that
Gwendolyn Nemphill is the one.

   I hope you find it in your heart
to grant Miss Nemphill a second chance
at life She deserves it!

   Thank you for your time and
consideration!

                    Respectfully Yours,

                    Sakara Varone
                    Reg# 74708-053
                    Federal Prison Camp
                    Route 37
                    Danbury CT 06811

Letter of recommendation for Gwendalyn Hemphill

November 9, 2010

Dear President Obama,

   I wish you could see the smile on my face and the tears building in my eyes as I speak about Gwendalyn Hemphill or Miss Gwen as she is known. I met her 11 months ago. Miss Gwen is truly a beautiful, kind and giving person. She works as a tutor and takes it "very" seriously! I have seen her stop what she was doing midstream to help a student or a woman in need. I personally have asked for her help, it was a 6 month commitment ... she said yes without needing to think it over. I feel truly blessed to have met such a wonderful person under such awful circumstances. When my 10 year old son saw her in the visiting room he said mom something is wrong with this country putting women in prison when their children need them but putting someone her age in prison is worse she's someone's grandma.

   Please have some compassion as you consider Miss Gwen for a pardon

Peacefully yours,
37482-038 Rita White

Cynthia N. Robertson #
63362053 federaL
Prison Camp 33 1/2
Pembroke Jtation
Danbury Ct 06811

Dear Mr. Rodgers,

I am writing this litter on behalf
of a woman I have grown to respect
as a Mother figure.

I have know Gwendolyn Hemphill for
four years. Mrs Gwendoly Hemphill and
I were roommates and she and I
have shared many thoughts about
our lives and our future. She has
been a role model for me and has
helped me with my GED. I am
praying that Mrs Hemphill will be
pardoned so that she can return
to her community to help other. She
is so patient and understanding.
and is willing to help anyone.
She wants to resume helping other
as she did before her incarceration.
                    Thank you
                    Cynthia N. Robertson
            # 63362053

11/11/10

Dear President Barack Obama:

My name is Christina Boykins, and I have know Mrs. Gwendolyn Hemphill for about 8 months. During that time, She has been a support system for me as well as others. I'm going to only speak for myself, and let you know that at times when I'm alone and missing the outside world, Mrs Gwen has always been there to offer me words of encouragement, and life long lessions. Mrs Gwen talks to me from her heart, but uses her experience to put it all in perspective for me. At times when I begin to question God, She's there, either at bible study, at Church, or just around the Camp assuring me that He's here, and all I have to do is believe and ask Him for the strength to get through this season. She is an active member in the Church, and every Sunday she recites special words from her heart, and I anticipate hearing what she has in store. I consider Mrs Gwen the most respected Women here at the Camp, and I'm blessed to have Come pass a Women of her Stature.

Sincerely yours
Christina Boykins 14831-052

Dear Mr. President,   11/11/2010
        My name is Marypal Morales and I
am currently is the federal prison. During
my stay here I had the pleasure to meet another inmate by the name of Gwendolyn
Hemphill. I have been incarcerated for 53
months in Danbury CT, but at the beginning
of my time I had a very hard time. Mrs.
Hemphill came in around that time and
when we first meet I was going into depression.
Mrs Hemphill was able to peell me out of this
depression regardless of her own worries. She
became my helper, my guidance, my support
through all this. She is my mentor and will
not let me give up. I am on my way out with a
sound mind thanks to Mrs. Hemphill, but I
leave with a big pain in my heart knowing that
a person like Mrs. Hemphill who all she does is
help everyone in this camp will still be here instead of being out of this place, out there helping people who need someone like her. Mrs.
Hemphill is very valuebal in this place, I can
imagine her out in this world. Mr. President
please consider Mrs. Hemphill. Thank you so
very much.
                    Marypal Morales
                  # 25524-038

Shahila N. Wallace   November 9, 2010
Federal Prison Camp
33½ Pembroke Station
Danbury, CT 06811

    I am currently incarcerated at Danbury's
Federal Prison Camp with Mrs. Gwendolyn Hemphill.
I have known Mrs. Hemphill since beginnings of
my stay. Mrs. Hemphill was the first to greet me when
coming here at Danbury with such a positive attitude.
She helped me around the camp as in finding what
I needed, where to go, and which direction to take.

    Each woman here at the camp has so much respect
for Mrs. Hemphill and here we refer to her as Mrs. Gwen.
It's never a day that goes by where she doesn't
have a smile on her face, and a uplifted spirit. You
will never no when she is down. Mrs. Hemphill always
stop to make sure you are oh, or whether it's
to say goodmorning, goodnight, or even how is
your day coming along.

    Mrs. Hemphill is a GED Education Tutor and
have helped many woman gain their GED which
graduation was recently held Friday November 5, 2010.
I shared a class with her which was "Starting
Your Own Business. She has inspired me to

Letters of Support
For Gwendolyn Hemphill
To Honorable Richard J. Leon

Excerpted From Her Sentencing
Memo Filed 6/15/06

748 Napoleon Street
Johnstown, PA 15901
(814) 539-5491
September 29, 2005

The Honorable Judge Richard J. Leon
US Federal Court
333 Constitution Avenue, NW
Washington, DC 20001

Honorable Judge Richard J. Leon,

My name is Alice Dorothy Taylor and I am a cousin of Gwendolyn Hemphill by marriage. I am 79 years of age and I have known Gwendolyn since her birth. In the absence of her mother, I have always tried to be like a mother to Gwen so I believe it is not unusual for me to petition you on her behalf. I think I am able to give insight to a side of Gwendolyn Hemphill that was probably not portrayed in the courtroom, but perhaps should be considered for the purposes of her sentencing; which is her personality.

Gwen's life has not been a crystal stair. You see, her mother passed away when she was one month old and she was raised by another aunt. This is the family that I too married into. Although I loved my husband very deeply, I was mocked by his family for being darker skinned. Gwendolyn was also met with a lot of resentment, which is one reason I have always felt close to her. She was frequently ostracized for being "ugly" and "skinny". I had the benefit of having a mother and father who loved me and raised me to be a proud woman so I was able to take the abuse, although it frequently broke my heart. However, Gwendolyn had no one to protect her from these hurtful insults. No one was there to go out of their way for Gwen. She was a motherless child.

The aunt who took Gwen in did as much as she was able to do for her. There were times when she was very young that I would bathe and clothe her and take her for walks. When she got a little older, she had to go to rummage sales to get clothes and shoes and there were times when others in the family would buy her an item here or there. In other words, her childhood survival depended on people "liking" Gwen. As you can well imagine, a "pleasing" type of personality emerged. It was very important for her to be liked by people because she generally felt that otherwise people were ashamed of her.

Your Honor, I submit to you that this is the most likely reason she is in the trouble she is in today. We like to think we grow out of these issues, but it is very possible and even likely for a painful and lonely childhood to affect the rest of our lives. It is probably the main reason for many of Gwen's successes, as well as her failures. For many of us, a childhood evokes happy memories. For Gwendolyn Hemphill, there is only sadness.

I can only imagine the difficulties you must face when making decisions regarding these types of sentences over people's lives. And I know it must be difficult to evaluate a person when you have only seen them in a courtroom setting. This is why I felt it was necessary to give you this information.

Letter to The Honorable Judge Richard J. Leon
Page 2

On her behalf, I would like to ask you to consider that (prior to this case) Gwendolyn Hemphill has never been in any sort of trouble with the law. I pray that you will also consider the previous years of servitude Mrs. Hemphill gave in serving other citizens. I strongly feel that, as in Heaven, a person's service to other people should count for something. Her possessions have already been taken from her. She has lost friendships. And she has lost her source of income. The media attention and public humiliation has caused her to lose the one thing that she has held on so tightly to for her survival all of these years; and that is the ability to be pleasing in the sight of others. This has certainly taken its toll on her. When you compare the life that Gwen Hemphill had built prior to this case, she has already lost so much. Gwen has already experienced a nervous breakdown many years ago. I pray it doesn't happen again.

I am a Christian woman and I am praying that God will lay it upon your heart to do His will. It was not an easy task for me to write this letter to you as it could very well bring up painful memories not only to Gwen and myself, but to family members who have since either changed their ways or don't have the humility to admit what they have (or have not) done. I only write this so that you may have an accurate picture of the person you will be sentencing. I humbly ask that you consider my statements when making your decision. May God continue to bless you and give you the strength do His will in performing your duties and making this and all decisions you make on behalf of our citizens.

Thank you so much for taking the time to read my plea.

Respectfully,

Alice D Taylor

Alice Dorothy Taylor

November 4, 2005

The Honorable Judge Richard J. Leon
U.S. Federal Court
333 Constitution Avenue, NW
Washington, DC 20001

Judge Leon: On December 8th you are scheduled to pass sentence on my wife Gwendolyn Hemphill. This is my plea to the Court to show leniency and mercy to a woman who, until this conviction, never violated the law in her entire 64 years. I surely, know this woman because I have been married to her for 46 of those years.

Your Honor, the person I heard described by the prosecutors is not the women I've known for all those years. Gwen is a kind, hardworking, generous person who never fails to give of her time and efforts in trying to help those in her family as well as others. She is a devoted wife and grandmother who wants nothing more than to love us and see to our needs. As my recent bout with prostate cancer will attest, I could not have survived the devastating implications of that disease were it not for Gwen's dedication and around the clock support and care. Even now with all of my other health challenges, the challenges of caring for a handicapped son and her own health problems, she places our care first with a patience and compassion that never ceases to amaze me.

The violation of law for which Gwendolyn was convicted is an aberration in her behavior and character and speaks more, in my view, to her efforts to please a superior than to an independent decision to simply perform illegal acts on behalf of others. Indeed, I was struck by the evidence that Gwen signed off on so many documents during the time in question. But clearly, as Special Assistant, Gwen, during Barbara Bullock's chronic absences, became the go- to person in the Washington Teachers Union offices for most decision making. My wife was overwhelmed by the load of work placed on her shoulders but continued to function like the loyal employee she had become. Because of this, the prosecution successfully had her appear to be the linchpin in this series of questionable acts. WTU had one ringleader and it was not Gwen Hemphill. Certainly, however, I acknowledge her mistakes and I believe in accountability. But I also pray that justice will be tempered with mercy.

My wife so concentrated on caring for her family that she delayed college until she reached her forties. Even now, I marvel at how she managed to accomplish such a goal with so many responsibilities on her shoulders. After receiving her degree she began to do community service with her sorority and her social organization. With that effort, she led the way in creating programs for abandoned babies left in hospitals by drug addicted and derelict mothers. My wife is an outstanding individual who has made a mistake and who has acknowledged her mistake and is very remorseful.

Your Honor, my wife is ill. She is diagnosed with asthma, hypertension, sciatica and arthritis of the spine which causes her constant pain and a slight limp. She is presently in physical therapy and periodically needs cortisone shots. Incarceration will only worsen her condition without the kind of care she currently receives here at home.

I respectfully ask that in your deliberations you take into full account the life of Gwendolyn Hemphill. I ask that she be given a length of probation or a suspended sentence commensurate to the crimes committed. I ask this on behalf of myself and my family. I ask mercy for Gwen Hemphill in the name of justice.

Sincerely,

Lawrence Hemphill

November 7, 2005

The Honorable Judge Richard J. Leon
U.S. Federal Court
333 Constitution Avenue, N.W.
Washington, D.C. 20011

Dear Honorable Judge Richard J. Leon;

My name is Barbara A. Brown, a very dear friend of Mrs. Gwendolyn Hemphill. I take this opportunity to address you with serious concern in regards to my friend Mrs. Hemphill. I met Mrs. Hemphill several years ago at the Mount Pleasant Baptist Church. She is an outstanding member in good standing with our church. She is a faithful bible study student and she also heads our Employment Ministry.

Mrs. Hemphill has demonstrated nothing but love to my daughter and I since meeting her and her family. It is with much sympathy and mercy that you would show **mercy** on Mrs. Hemphill. Honorable Judge with all due respect we have been praying together to Almighty God for strength, good health and guidance to endure for what's ahead for my sister in Christ, Mrs. Hemphill. I believe in my heart, body and soul that the God we serve and worship is a (**Just & Faithful God**). God does forgive us for sins committed unknowingly, only when we sincerely repent and feel so sorrowful for our sins and we all fall short of the glory of God as well.

Honorable Judge as we continue to pray, it is my sincere prayer that you would have **mercy and grace upon Mrs. Hemphill. Also please take into consideration Mrs. Hemphill's age as well.** I believe a person is **not** responsible for situations or circumstances that occur unknowingly, it is just apart of life that we go through.

Again, with all due respect your Honor from the bottom of your heart please grant unto Mrs. Hemphill **mercy** in your court room whenever the time presents itself for her to stand before you. Again, please have **mercy** on Mrs. Gwendolyn Hemphill in the name of Jesus.

Thanking you in advance for your cooperation in this matter, it is greatly appreciated.

Sincerely yours,

Barbara A. Brown

Barbara A. Brown

Theme: A Deeper Concern for our Church and Community

Mount Pleasant Baptist Church

215 Rhode Island Avenue, N.W.
Washington, D.C. 20001

BOARD OF DEACONS
Henry T. Sellers, Chairman
202-865-1215

BOARD OF TRUSTEES
Claude A. Gregory, Chairman
301-650-9112

Rev. Terry D. Streeter, Pastor

3701 Endicott Place
Springdale, Maryland 20774
STUDY: (202) 332-5748   RES: (301) 341-0621

CHURCH CLERK
LaVerne Harvey
202-575-2245

PASTOR'S SECRETARY
Paulette Sellers
301-630-7254

October 5, 2005

The Honorable Judge Richard J. Leon
U.S. Federal Court
333 Constitution Avenue, NW
Washington, DC 20001

Dear Judge Leon:

I write in support of Gwendolyn Hemphill, who will be sentenced in your court on December 8, 2005. I am Mrs. Hemphill's Pastor at Mt. Pleasant Baptist Church. Mrs. Hemphill united with our church in June of 1990 and since that time, has been a faithful member and one who has exemplified tremendous Christian character. Even throughout this ordeal in her life, she has remained faithful and committed to helping others.

Mrs. Hemphill is a Trustee of Mt. Pleasant Baptist Church. Although she is on leave of absence from the Board of Trustees because of her legal struggles, she is still a vital member of the Board. Mrs. Hemphill also headed our Employment Ministry at the church where she has helped many people find meaningful employment. She was the architect of our summer jobs program where through the giving of the membership, we were able to employ many young people during the summer. My own daughter has benefited from Mrs. Hemphill's work in this area. On April 8, 2005, our church received the President's Outstanding Contribution Award from the Greater Washington Urban League for our summer jobs for youth program. While it was given to our church, it really was Gwendolyn Hemphill's award for she made it all happen.

There are many, many members of our church who have been blessed by Mrs. Hemphill's help. She has prayed with others and been with them in their time of need. Even in my own personal crisis, Mrs. Hemphill stood by me. She is a faithful Bible Class attendee and she is a part of one of our discipleship groups. In 2003, I had the pleasure of baptizing her husband, Lawrence Hemphill. Both of them have been loyal members of our congregation.

There are countless community service projects that Mrs. Hemphill has spearheaded. Most notably among them was the "Boarder Babies". And more recently, Mrs. Hemphill has worked with the CSOSA/Faith Based Collaborative dealing with prisoner reentry into the community.

I realize that Mrs. Hemphill has been convicted of serious crimes for which she is very remorseful. While we cannot change what has happened, I do beg you for mercy in her sentencing.

Not only had she led an exemplary life prior to these events, she has done many good things for people throughout her life. These are the kinds of things that cause me to seek your mercy. I commit the resources of our congregation to aid in counseling her and helping her in this time of need. I am a firm believer that Mrs. Hemphill deserves another chance. The Mt. Pleasant Baptist congregation as well as the Streeter family is committed to seeing it through.

I thank you for your consideration and know that the will of God will surely be done. If you need to speak directly to me, please feel free to call me at the above listed numbers. God's blessings upon you.

Sincerely,

Rev. Perry D. Streeter

Greater Washington Urban League, Inc.

Empowering Communities. Changing Lives.

November 7, 2005

Maudine R. Cooper
President & CEO

The Honorable Judge Richard J. Leon
U.S. Federal Court
333 Constitution Avenue, NW
Washington, DC 20001

Dear Judge Leon:

I am President and CEO of the Greater Washington Urban League. I write this letter in support of Gwendolyn Hemphill, who will be sentenced in your court on December 8, 2005. I have known Mrs. Hemphill since 1984, approximately 22 years. I know that Mrs. Hemphill has been convicted of a serious crime, and I am still in shock. This behavior is not the Gwen Hemphill that I know. She has always devoted her life to her family and helping those less fortunate.

Mrs. Hemphill is best know for her outstanding fundraising efforts to provide a home for those babies abandoned by their crack-addicted mothers. That home has been operating at Meigs Place, NE for 15 years or more. She also worked with teenage girls to educate them about teenage pregnancy and to encourage them to stay in school and get a quality education. She has been the catalyst in a summer jobs program with the Greater Washington Urban League which earned her church the GWUL President's Outstanding Contribution Award from our organization.

Mrs. Hemphill has always volunteered to assist others in the community - from feeding the homeless to serving Thanksgiving dinners to senior citizens. She has always stepped in to volunteer and been a dedicated government worker as well as a committed citizen. Until her recent conviction I have never known her to be involved in any type of crime, and as stated above, I am in shock.

I ask that you show mercy as you undertake your sentencing decision. Hopefully, you will give Mrs. Hemphill the opportunity to continue to serve others as she has so faithfully done for many years and view the behaviors for which she was convicted as aberrations.

Sincerely,

Maudine R. Cooper

2901 Fourteenth Street, N.W.
Washington, DC 20009
(202) 265-8200
FAX (202) 265-6122
E-Mail:LUWGDBS@aol.com
Website www.gwul.org

fpi

focus point international

November 4, 2005

Honorable Judge Richard Leon
United States District Court Judge
United States District Court
333 Constitution Avenue, NW
Washington, DC 20001

Dear Honorable Richard Leon:

I am writing to offer my unconditional support of Mrs. Gwendolyn Hemphill (Case # 03-516). I am President/CEO of a human service consultant firm, Focus Point International, located in Washington, D.C. Focus Point is a private service organization committed to promoting self-sufficiency among individuals and families who are considered "at risk".

I served as Mrs. Hemphill's supervisor with a faith-based organization. During her tenure with our organization Mrs. Hemphill was a model employee, who required no supervision. She was a self-starter and was task oriented. She was committed to the completion of every task with proficiency and in a timely manner. There were many times when I have requested Mrs. Hemphill representation at meetings and conferences on my behalf. She exhibited professionalism at all times whether in a personal or professional environment.

At Focus Point we employ consultants to provide life skills and job readiness training to our clients. We have contracts with alternative schools, non-profit community based organizations, corporate organizations and faith-based institutions. I am truly impressed with Mrs. Hemphill's work ethic and skills. Therefore, I have asked Mrs. Hemphill to join our firm as a consultant. I am aware of her felony convictions and the seriousness of her charges. I am also aware of her remorse and willingness to accept responsibility for her actions.

I believe Mrs. Hemphill's restitution for her crime can best be served with an alternative to confinement I am confident that Mrs. Hemphill will add a value to the community from this experience. Honorable Judge Leon, I plead with all my heart for you to choose an alternative to incarceration for Mrs. Hemphil

Thank you for your consideration and compassion in this request.

Sincerely,

Diane Sims-Moore, President/CEO
Focus Point International

10 October 2005

The Honorable Judge Richard J. Leon
U.S. Federal Court
333 Constitution Avenue, NW
Washington, DC 20001

Dear Judge Leon:

Subject: Mrs Gwendolyn Hemphill

I have known Mrs Gwendolyn Hemphill for approximately 9 years on a personal and professional level. I have worked with Mrs Hemphill, where she was an officer manager for a firm. She welcomed me to the firm with open arms and helped me settle into my position as a receptionist.

Gwendolyn has a big heart. She is loyal, caring, loving and is always helping others before helping herself. In addition to her being a wonderful grandmother, mother, leader, sister, mentor and friend to her own family she is always extending those same roles to persons like myself who needed a mother, mentor or a friend at some point of their lives.

I am a legal secretary in a prestigious firm in Bermuda, and without Gwendolyn's compassion, direction and understanding to help me along the of path of life, it would have probably taken me much longer to achieve my goals. She always firmly stressed the importance of work ethics. One never really knows how much a hug or a "I love you" can do for someone; sometimes, that's all they need. I admire Gwendolyn for her sincerity, dependability and honesty just to name a few of her wonderful qualities of being a humanitarian.

In summary, I know that Mrs. Hemphill has been convicted of serious crimes but I am asking you to give her another opportunity to serve her community. your judgement She is not a person who is dangerous to the community. If anything she is an asset to the community and it would be a great loss for her family and others who look up to her.

Sincerely,

Tina Wynn

September 22, 2005
The Honorable Richard J. Leon
333 Constitution Avenue, N.W.
Washington, D.C. 20001

RE: Gwendolyn Hemphill

Dear Judge Leon:

I write this letter on behalf of Mrs. Gwendolyn M. Hemphill who is to be sentenced by your court on December 8, 2005. As a resident of the District of Columbia, as one who knows Mrs. Hemphill well, and as a neighbor, I come now to ask for the court's lenience and compassion as such relates to the "sentencing" phase.

Your Honor, I met Mrs. Hemphill and her family some 30 years ago. Several years after that she began her crusade to educate the public on the plight of our city's Border Babies who are babies born to crack addicted Mothers. For years she attended civic meetings, church functions, advocacy gatherings, and made radio appearances to garner support for the little children who could not speak for nor help themselves. Because of her deep and unswerving humanitarian outreach and concomitant fundraising efforts, Mrs. Hemphill raised over $85,000 to secure a home for these Babies. Surely, her goodness shall follow her all the days of her life.

In the mid 1970s I witnessed Ms. Hemphill's civic outreach again as each of us was intimately involved in the discussion and pre-construction phase of the Metro Green Line which runs thru our inner-city. The critical issue surrounding said discussion was "whose and how many homes" would have to be destroyed to facilitate construction of the Green Line. Gwendolyn Hemphill's constant refrain was that inner-city residents had worked hard and had made great sacrifices to buy their homes. Therefore, government must study every feasible option for said construction and that citizens' homes did not have to be razed. The Metro Board eventually agreed with Ms. Hemphill's admonition; the Green Line was built; and no homes was destroyed.

Your Honor, over the course of some three decades I have worked with Ms Hemphill on behalf of many social, civic, and charitable organizations. At every station along the way she made great sacrifices to serve and to help the least important among us. Raising scholarship funds for underprivileged children, collecting clothing for the needy, visiting nursing homes to assist the elderly, and working with faith-based institutions are some of the demonstrable examples of Ms Hemphill's life-long advocacy.

I realize that Mrs. Hemphill made mistakes, and in my conversations with her over the past three years she has shown great remorse. On behalf of Mrs. Hemphill who has done so much for so many citizens for so long, I beseech you, Sir, and your honorable court to weigh her goodness against her lapse in judgment.

Respectfully Submitted,

Norman C. Neverson

Norman C. Neverson

Neighbor
Former Teacher-DCPS
Former Chair-Advisory Neighbor Commissioner ANC 4-D
Former Chair-(NUSH)Neighbors United to Save Our Homes
Former Chair-NAACP Youth Division

ABOUT THE AUTHOR

Gwendolyn Hemphill born and raised in Johnstown, Pennsylvania, during the post Great Depression era, is a motivational speaker and a prison reform activist. This modern-day freedom fighter utilizes her prolific experiences and her voice to advocate for the rights of incarcerated women.

From humble beginnings in a small rural town, Hemphill worked relentlessly to overcome barriers of racism and poverty, moving to Washington D.C. in the 60's to provide a better life for her family. Gaining a notable position at the White House under the Carter administration in the 70's, Hemphill utilized her keen wit, business savvy and political connections to help make waves in employment opportunities for African Americans in the White House.

Hemphill, a Political Science graduate of Howard University, has provided sizable contributions to the Washington D.C. community as a strong political advocate. Combining forces with various community groups and political organizations such as the legendary Student Nonviolent Coordinating Committee (SNCC) to serving as the President of the D.C. chapter of the Coalition of 100 Black Women, Hemphill worked vigorously for over three decades to create change.

After her retirement from the District of Columbia Mayor's office in 2001, Hemphill was offered a position at the Washington

Teachers Union (WTU). Blinded by her ambitious desire to reign once again as a top political socialite, she made a poor choice that ended her career and destroyed her stellar reputation, costing her a 11 year prison sentence as a first time, non-violent offender.

Through her powerful message, Hemphill illustrates the hardships and circumstances encountered by women, such as herself, who have been sentenced to over a decade in federal prison. She selflessly exposes her own mistakes and character flaws to warn her audience about the detriment of poor choices, urging them to avoid shortcuts at all cost!

Voices International Publications Presents

$\mathcal{V}oices$ of CONSEQUENCES
ENRICHMENT SERIES
CREATED BY: JAMILA T. DAVIS

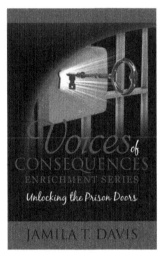

Unlocking the Prison Doors: 12 Points to Inner Healing and Restoration

ISBN: 978-09855807-4-2 Textbook
ISBN: 978-09855807-5-9 Workbook/Journal
ISBN: 978-09855807-6-6 Curriculum Guide

is a nondenominational, faith-based instructional manual created to help incarcerated women gain inner healing and restoration. In a comforting voice that readers can recognize and understand, this book provides the tools women need to get past the stage of denial and honestly assess their past behavioral patterns, their criminal conduct and its impact on their lives and others. It provides a platform for women to begin a journey of self-discovery, allowing them to assess the root of their problems and dilemmas and learn how to overcome them.

This book reveals real-life examples and concrete strategies that inspire women to release anger, fear, shame and guilt and embrace a new world of opportunities.

After reading readers will be empowered to release the inner shackles and chains that have been holding them bound and begin to soar in life!

INTERNATIONAL PUBLICATIONS
"Changing Lives One Page At A Time."
www.vocseries.com

Voices International Publications Presents

$\mathcal{V}oices$ of
CONSEQUENCES
ENRICHMENT SERIES
CREATED BY: JAMILA T. DAVIS

Permission to Dream: 12 Points to Discovering Your Life's Purpose and Recapturing Your Dreams

ISBN: 978-09855807-4-2 Textbook
ISBN: 978-09855807-5-9 Workbook/Journal
ISBN: 978-09855807-6-6 Curriculum Guide

is a nondenominational, faith-based, instruction manual created to inspire incarcerated women to discover their purpose in life and recapture their dreams. In a way readers can identify with and understand, this book provides strategies they can use to overcome the stigma and barriers of being an ex-felon.
This book reveals universal laws and proven self-help techniques that successful people apply in their everyday lives. It helps readers identify and destroy bad habits and criminal thinking patterns, enabling them to erase the defilement of their past. Step-by-step this book empowers readers to recognize their talents and special skill sets, propelling them to tap into the power of "self" and discover their true potential, and recapture their dreams.
After reading , readers will be equipped with courage and tenacity to take hold of their dreams and become their very best!

INTERNATIONAL PUBLICATIONS
"Changing Lives One Page At A Time."
www.vocseries.com

Voices International Publications Presents

$\mathcal{V}oices$ of
CONSEQUENCES
ENRICHMENT SERIES
CREATED BY: JAMILA T. DAVIS

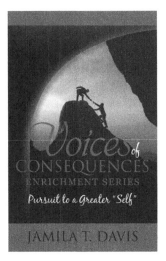

Pursuit to A Greater "Self:" 12 Points to Developing Good Character and HealthyRelationships

ISBN: 978-09855807-7-3 Textbook
ISBN: 978-09855807-8-0 Workbook/Journal
ISBN: 978-09855807-9-7 Curriculum Guide

is a non-denominational, faith-based, instruction manual created to help incarcerated women develop good character traits and cultivate healthy relationships. This book is filled with real-life examples that illustrate how good character traits have helped many people live a more prosperous life, and how deficient character has caused others to fail. These striking examples, along with self-help strategies revealed in this book, are sure to inspire women to dethrone bad character traits and develop inner love, joy, peace, patience, kindness, generosity, faithfulness, gentleness and self-control. This book also instructs women how to utilize these positive character traits to cultivate healthy relationships.

After reading readers will be inspired to let their light shine for the world to see that true reformation is attainable, even after imprisonment!

INTERNATIONAL PUBLICATIONS
"Changing Lives One Page At A Time."
www.vocseries.com

ORDER FORM

Mail to: 196-03 Linden Blvd.
St. Albans, NY 11412
or visit us on the web @
www.vocseries.com

QTY	Title	Price
	Unlocking the Prison Doors	14.95
	Unlocking the Prison Doors Workbook/Journal	14.95
	Permission to Dream	14.95
	Permission to Dream Workbook/Journal	14.95
	Pursuit to A Greater "Self"	14.95
	Pursuit to A Greater "Self" Workbook/Journal	14.95
	The High Price I Had To Pay	7.99
	The High Price I Had To Pay 2	7.99
	The High Price I Had To Pay 3	9.99
	Total For Books	
	20% Inmate Discount -	
	Shipping/Handling +	
	Total Cost	

* Shipping/Handling 1-3 books 4.95
     4-9 books 8.95
* Incarcerated individuals receive a 20% discount on each book purchase.
* Forms of Accepted Payments: Certified Checks, Institutional Checks and Money Orders.
* Bulk rates are available upon requests for orders of 10 books or more.
* Curriculum Guides are available for group sessions.
* All mail-in orders take 5-7 business days to be delivered. For prison orders, please allow
  up to (3) three weeks for delivery.

SHIP TO:
Name: _____
Address: _____

_____

_____

City: _____

State: _____ Zip: _____